breathe

M000309105

BABYLON

participant's guide

Shawna Songer Gaines

BEACON HILL PRESS
OF KANSAS CITY

CONTENTS

WELCOME

Thank you for joining us on this journey through *Breathe: Babylon*, by Shawna Songer Gaines. If you haven't gone through a *Breathe* study before, we are delighted to welcome you to your first one. If you are a *Breathe* Bible study veteran, then we are pleased to welcome you back!

We'd like to start by explaining the concepts of biblical theology and hermeneutics, upon which the *Breathe* studies are based.

Biblical theology is a lens for reading Scripture that is set to look for the big story God is telling throughout history. Biblical theology places scripture in conversation with scripture and assumes that every book tells a different perspective of the same story—a story the church is still telling today.

As we study Scripture through the lens of biblical theology, we use another tool, hermeneutics. Hermeneutics is simply a way to explain or interpret Scripture. The three hermeneutical questions we will ask in each lesson are:

1. What do you learn about the character of God?

2. What do you learn about what God is up to in the world—both in the world of Scripture and in our world today?

3. How can we join God's work in the world?

These three questions help us reflect on each passage of Scripture. The questions we ask reveal the lens through which we see God and read Scripture. These questions assume at least three things:

1. God is the primary character in all of Scripture.

2. God's actions are consistent with God's character, which never changes.

3. God calls us to be part of the work God is doing in the world.

As we study Scripture, we must also understand its inspiration. We believe Scripture is the inspired word of God. In fact, we believe it is God-breathed. While it is important that we study and dig into Scripture to learn more about who God is and what God is up to, it is just as important that we always approach Scripture in the power of the Spirit. That is why this participant's guide includes prompts for prayer and allows space to write. These practices help open us up to the Spirit who breathed into the biblical writers and breathes inspiration and revelation into God's people of every generation.

Finally, we need to understand the echoes from scripture to scripture. Because Scripture is breathed by the Holy Spirit, there are echoes of themes that reveal God's character. Even though there is an incredible variety of biblical genres and authors, and even though the Bible was written over a span of roughly 1,500 years, the same images of God's character ring throughout the pages from Genesis to Revelation. The Babylon motif echoes across Scripture because God is calling us to form new visions for ourselves and our communities.

As you work through this study, you may want to refer to this introduction from time to time, to help you recall the tools of biblical theology and hermeneutics.

HOW TO USE THIS PARTICIPANT'S GUIDE

This guide is intended for you to use on your own time, between group sessions. In order for each group meeting to generate maximum discussion and learning potential, the idea is for you to complete each chapter of this study before its corresponding group meeting. Each chapter has been written in such a way that is intended to prepare you for your next group meeting without spoiling the content.

You may complete all or part of each chapter as you feel comfortable, and in whatever time frame works best for you. Do not feel pressured to complete a full chapter all at once, or to answer every single question in every chapter, or even to proceed in a linear fashion!

Some of the questions, especially surrounding the scriptures, may require some background awareness or foreknowledge of biblical stories; others won't. Some questions may make more sense after their corresponding group sessions. Or your group discussions and some of the things Shawna says in the videos may give you new insight into some of the questions asked here. That's okay. Work through it at your own pace.

This guide is designed to meet you wherever you are in your faith journey. The one thing we recommend as you work through this participant's guide is to read the introduction paragraphs before your group sessions. They will directly lead and tie in to the content you will receive from the videos in your group meetings.

We want you to use this guide in the way that works best for you, while remaining open to stretching yourself and growing outside your comfort zone. We pray that you are part of a group where you feel safe being vulnerable enough to grow and that this study facilitates such opportunities. Blessings to you, and may God do a great work in you as you study *Breathe: Babylon*.

1   THE CITY

∽ INTRODUCTION

Babylon is a character that plays a significant role in Scripture, appearing as early as Genesis and as late as Revelation—and many places in between. The city of Babylon often has a negative connotation, but why? It is the historical birthplace of civilization. It is alive and teeming with activity. The city is not an inherently bad place, but Babylon is so much more than a city. It is a way of life that allows and encourages us to put ourselves at the center of everything. God isn't afraid of Babylon, and God isn't absent from Babylon. From the beginning of time until now, God has been moving among God's people to bring about their redemption.

{ **Genesis 11; Jeremiah 5**

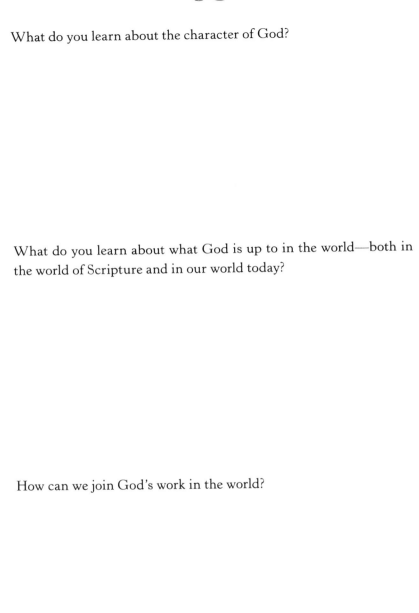

What do you learn about the character of God?

What do you learn about what God is up to in the world—both in the world of Scripture and in our world today?

How can we join God's work in the world?

ᕙ BREATHE IN THE WORD

Genesis 11:4. What is the significance of the people's commitment to building the tower?

Genesis 18:20, Jeremiah 5:1. What do these scriptural echoes tell you about the character of God's people? What do they tell you about the character of God?

Jeremiah 5:29. Through Jeremiah, God accuses the people of no longer having the marks that set them apart—relying on God, doing good, seeking justice, defending the poor. What is your reaction to God wanting to punish God's own people?

ᕦ PRAYER

God of provision, I have more than enough in you, but it can be easy to be tempted into thinking I need more, more, more. Help me reclaim the marks in my life of being your hands and feet in the world—focusing on others rather than focusing on what I can build or do for myself. Help me to orient my life toward you and your people, rather than toward myself and my own abilities.

❧ MEDITATE

When we think about idolatry it's often hard for us to make the connection to our lives today. We might conjure up images of golden calves or human sacrifice. In Babylon we see not only a city of idolatry but also things we can more easily relate to—excessive consumption, hubris, and self-reliance. How do we know when and if we have fallen to the temptation to make ourselves the center of our own story? The Bible tells us that where our treasure is, that's where our heart will be. Treasure isn't always one specific thing. It's often a combination of how we spend our time, talents, and resources.

Are we spending our resources to pursue the marks of God's people—goodness, justice, mercy, love, humility? Or have we become intoxicated by the desire to pilot our own destinies, and neglected the work God is calling us to do in the world?

⌇ CHALLENGE: TIME BUDGET

Do you know where your treasure is? Are you exalting your own creativity, piloting your own destiny, pulling yourself up by your bootstraps? One way to help us determine our treasure is to look at how we spend our time.

Pick at least one day this week and keep close track of how you spend your time. If you work all day, don't just write down that you were at work from 8:00 until 5:00. Try to break things down into hour-long increments (or even shorter!), from the time you got up to the time you finally put down your phone and went to sleep.

Scrutinizing your routine can reveal where you may be missing opportunities to spend intentional time with God, learning to rely on God.

Are you surprised by any revelations about how you spend your time? Are there any obvious needs to re-prioritize your time to shift the focus away from yourself? How might you do that in the coming week?

❧ NOTES

Video sessions are available for individual purchase and download at www.BreatheSeries.com.

The City 15

2 | EXILE

∾ INTRODUCTION

Have you ever pray-wept? We find examples of pray-weeping in the biblical Psalms. Psalm 137 is the biblical version of reality TV. It is the song of a people experiencing a true and painful exile in Babylon, and all of creation sings their song. If tears have ever been your only prayer, you're in good company.

Remember that the Israelites are reaping in Babylon what they sowed in Jerusalem. A kingdom built by human hands—though it may have begun in covenant, as Israel did, with Abraham—often ends up existing to serve itself rather than others. The people of the kingdom of Israel have begun to worship their own kingdom and the works of their own hands to such an extent that they find themselves in exile in Babylon—where the only thing they can do is cry out for salvation.

{ **Psalm 137**
Matthew 1:1–17

What do you learn about the character of God?

What do you learn about what God is up to in the world—both in the world of Scripture and in our world today?

How can we join God's work in the world?

∾ BREATHE IN THE WORD

Psalm 137. What emotions emerge for you when you read this lament? What is gained through expressing lament?

∾ PRAYER

All-encompassing God, you meet me wherever I am because you are already there. You exist in my joy and in my sorrow. Through your power and mercy you provide a safe place to express my deepest emotions. Help me be honest with myself and with you when I am in periods of exile and suffering. Through your Spirit, minister to me when I walk through the valley of the shadow of death. Remind me of your presence, and make me aware that your mercies are new each day.

The Israelites in exile in Babylon sit down and weep when they realize how far from the Promised Land they have strayed. Israel's Promised Land was designed to be a manifestation of God's covenant with God's people.

How has God's covenant relationship manifested itself in your own life? How have you felt God calling you to a place where you can use your unique gifts in a way that manifests God's presence? Maybe it's a vision for how you can work toward justice in the world. Maybe it's speaking truth on an issue you're passionate about. Maybe it's being a support system for someone who desperately needs it.

Or maybe you're searching, clinging to the covenant relationship you know you formed with God, but right now you're feeling separated from God. Maybe you've been in the Promised Land but where you are now feels more like exile.

Wherever you are, God is there—even if you, like the Israelites, don't feel like that's true right now. It's okay to throw up your hands, to cry out, to acknowledge when you're in a place of joyless exile.

∾ CHALLENGE: CREATE

The Psalms come in a variety of genres, the most common being psalms of lament, psalms of thanksgiving, and psalms of praise. In any genre, the Psalms give us encouragement and permission to cry out to God no matter what we're feeling.

Read through some psalms of lament: Psalm 3, 22, 137, 142.

Read through some psalms of thanksgiving: Psalm 100, 107, 118, 138.

Read through some psalms of praise: Psalm 8, 19, 145, 146.

You might notice that many psalms incorporate more than one of the three named elements. Write out your own psalm to God that reflects where you are in your life's journey. If lament resonates with you right now, practice incorporating praise or thanksgiving (or both!) after you've expressed your lament.

∾ NOTES

_____

_____

_____

_____

_____

_____

_____

_____

_____

_____

_____

_____

_____

_____

_____

_____

_____

_____

_____

_____

3 | SET APART

∽ INTRODUCTION

God's people have made mistakes in their covenant relationship; they have accepted their exile to Babylon. And now, God says through Jeremiah, they're supposed to make the most of it. God tells them in Jeremiah 29 to seek the welfare of the city, to seek the good of the very people causing their lament!

Daniel is brought to be installed as an officer in service to the king. The idea behind promoting conquered exiles like Daniel and his friends to positions that Babylon considers honorable is that, if you treat exiles well enough, they won't incite a revolt against your kingdom. They will instead, as Shawna likes to say in the videos, become "good Babylonians." So it seems that God's call to seek the welfare of the city and Babylon's invitation to be good citizens are in harmony with each other. But Daniel knows there is one crucial difference, and that involves who is really in charge. Daniel's faithfulness allows God to use him to enact God's message of love and justice in the world.

{ **Daniel 1**
Jeremiah 1:1–11

What do you learn about the character of God?

What do you learn about what God is up to in the world—both in the world of Scripture and in our world today?

How can we join God's work in the world?

◌◌ BREATHE IN THE WORD

Jeremiah 29:11. How does your understanding of this verse change when you read verses 1–10 first?

Daniel 1:6–7. What is the significance of Daniel and his companions receiving new names at the court of King Nebuchadnezzar?

∽ PRAYER

Oh God, you call me to balance myself delicately between embedding myself in the world and maintaining my unique mark as your follower. You prepare a path for me; help me to see the way forward when I face difficult decisions or circumstances. Give me your grace as I heed your call to serve you more faithfully and to minister to my community more actively.

∽ MEDITATE

It sounds like a paradox to be set apart yet join God's work in the world. The church struggles to determine the proper relationship between purity and engagement. Sometimes we draw our lines of separation from culture so far back that we aren't willing to advocate for the least of these, to get in the trenches with the suffering, to be the voice of the voiceless. Other times we engage so much in the world that we forget how to be set apart and others cannot distinguish us as God's people. Often we struggle to sit exactly in the middle of these two extremes.

Which side of the tension do you tend to fall on more often in your life? What opportunities are available to you right now that would help you balance the scales so that you are appropriately *set apart* in order to *serve* the world around you?

෨෨ CHALLENGE: SEEK THE GOOD

Think about what it would look like to seek the good of your community beyond your usual sphere of influence. Maybe there is a particular need in your neighborhood; maybe your church offers outreach opportunities; maybe you can partner with a local non-profit to share your resources.

Try to focus on opportunities to build bridges and relationships. There are plenty of ways you can serve for one day or give money once to a cause, but restoration and renewal so often happen through established relationships. Challenge yourself to take the first step outside your comfort zone by seeking opportunities for long-term, sustained community.

Video sessions are available for individual purchase and download at www.BreatheSeries.com.

ᦟ NOTES

_____

_____

_____

_____

_____

_____

_____

_____

_____

_____

_____

_____

_____

_____

_____

_____

_____

_____

_____

_____

_____

_____

4 | TRUTH

ᔆᕤ INTRODUCTION

In Daniel 1, we read about how God rewarded Daniel's faithfulness to God by protecting him from the judgment of the king and advancing his position in the Babylonian kingdom. As Daniel's story continues in chapter 2, we find King Nebuchadnezzar seeking someone who can accurately interpret his dreams. And we find Daniel facing another opportunity to display his faith in the God who has not abandoned him in exile.

{ **Genesis 39–41 (skim)
Daniel 2**

What do you learn about the character of God?

What do you learn about what God is up to in the world—both in the world of Scripture and in our world today?

How can we join God's work in the world?

Genesis 39–41. After skimming these passages in conjunction with Daniel 2, what echoes of Joseph's story do you see occurring in Daniel's story?

Daniel 2:26–28. How do Daniel's actions interrupt the king's self-seeking behavior?

Daniel 2:46–49. How could this scenario have played out badly for Daniel? What does Daniel's commitment to the truth tell you about faith and about God?

ᕦᕤ PRAYER

God of wisdom, give me your revelation of the truth, for myself and for creation. Tune me to your heart for creation, that I may be a relevant voice seeking the good of the city. I empty myself before you, that you may fill me up with your light so that I may take that light into the world.

∾ MEDITATE

> God is the origin of everything good we see in the world. We are called to join God's work in bringing these attributes to the world. Spend a moment meditating on the verses Shawna uses to close out each session:
>
> "Finally, beloved, whatever is true, whatever is honorable, whatever is just, whatever is pure, whatever is pleasing, whatever is commendable, if there is any excellence and if there is anything worthy of praise, think about these things. Keep on doing the things that you have learned and received and heard and seen in me, and the God of peace will be with you."
> —Philippians 4:8–9, NRSV
>
> Ask God to show you what these things are in your life so that you can praise and thank God for them. Then humbly ask what areas in your life could use an infusion of God's truth and beauty.

∾ CHALLENGE: PURSUE HUMILITY

As you pursue humility this week, symbolize your search with your spiritual practice: Try kneeling, sitting, or lying down on the floor to pray as an acknowledgment to God and a reminder to yourself of who is the source of good things.

Video sessions are available for individual purchase and download at www.BreatheSeries.com.

NOTES

_____

_____

_____

_____

_____

_____

_____

_____

_____

_____

_____

_____

_____

_____

_____

_____

_____

_____

_____

5 | DELIVERANCE

⌇ INTRODUCTION

As Daniel continues to act in ways that ingratiate him to the king, we are shown in chapter 3 a story about his three friends following the example of faithfulness to God that Daniel has already set in chapters 1 and 2. Then in Daniel 6, we again see Daniel choosing faithfulness to God over the strong temptation of Babylon. Daniel and his friends learn about the importance of God's deliverance *in* exile rather than deliverance *from* exile.

{ Daniel 3; Daniel 6

What do you learn about the character of God?

What do you learn about what God is up to in the world—both in the world of Scripture and in our world today?

How can we join God's work in the world?

∽ BREATHE IN THE WORD

Daniel 3:1, 7. What scriptural echoes do you hear in this story about worshiping a golden statue?

Daniel 3:18. What is implied by the statement that starts, "But if not . . ."? What is the significance of that implication?

Daniel 3:30. What is the significance, or what are the implications, of this verse?

Daniel 6:14, 16. Why does the king try to rescue Daniel, against his own edict? What does King Darius mean when he tells Daniel that he hopes Daniel's God delivers him?

Daniel 3:28; 6:26–28. Why do you think these stories have similar endings despite featuring different kings?

God, in the moments I should be most alone, you are with me. Remind me of your continued presence; teach me to look for that presence, to be attuned to finding your Spirit in my everyday interactions. May this knowledge give me the boldness to stand for true goodness in the world by bowing to you and only you.

∾ MEDITATE

Sometimes Christians might feel like the week culminates on Sunday, with a list of things (like "go to church!") we have checked off as having done in the last week. But church—being with other believers and practicing worship—is where our week should *start*. Church is where we begin to learn to move in the direction God has called us, but it is just that—a beginning. The real dance of salvation occurs in the world, in our communities, as we join God's work in the world.

Consider how to shift your focus from viewing Sunday as a culmination of your week to viewing Sunday and weekly church attendance as the catalyst that helps you prioritize the work of God in the world throughout the upcoming week.

∾ CHALLENGE: REORIENTING WORSHIP

What is one thing that keeps you from a fuller expression of worship? Maybe you have a hard time practicing stillness with God. Maybe you forget to pray throughout the day. Maybe you are self-conscious about expressing your faith in your daily life.

This week, focus on one thing that may distract you from worshiping God, and actively practice ways to remedy this distraction. Whatever your challenge is, try to find points throughout your day when you can counteract the challenge to create new worship habits.

❦ NOTES

_____

_____

_____

_____

_____

_____

_____

_____

_____

_____

_____

_____

_____

_____

_____

_____

_____

Video sessions are available for individual purchase and download at www.BreatheSeries.com.

6 | CRUMBLING KINGDOM

೪ INTRODUCTION

The kingdom of Babylon is crumbling. When we left Daniel in chapter 3, Nebuchadnezzar was still firmly in charge, but in chapter 4, Nebuchadnezzar is driven to insanity and then humbled before God. His humiliation leads him to an important realization about who God really is.

In Daniel 5, Nebuchadnezzar's descendant Belshazzar sits on the throne, but Belshazzar hasn't learned from his predecessor's experiences. We find him throwing a party and getting drunk from wine served out of the golden vessels of the Israelite temple, taken during the conquest.

{ Daniel 5

What do you learn about the character of God?

What do you learn about what God is up to in the world—both in the world of Scripture and in our world today?

How can we join God's work in the world?

ᘓᗢ BREATHE IN THE WORD

Daniel 5:2–4. What is revealed about Belshazzar when he brings out golden vessels previously used in Israel's temple worship?

Daniel 5:29–30. What scriptural echoes do you see between this story and our previous Daniel stories with King Nebuchadnezzar and King Darius? What is different this time about Daniel's promotions from the king?

∾ PRAYER

God, you call to me from the past with words that apply to my present in order to bring about a more holy and just future. Help me to hear this call and be encouraged that you are still sovereign. Lead me into humility, that I may carry the message of your kingdom to a world that desperately needs it.

∾ MEDITATE

Often we feel like the only realities of life are our day-to-day experiences—our jobs, our bills, our families, our pain. Yes, our daily lives are absolutely real, but we offer no hope for the world we serve if they are the only reality we are aware of. Consider that we are called to be part of a new kingdom that has come and is coming still. Seek what God is telling you about how to live this flesh-and-blood reality in service to your community.

✑ CHALLENGE: FAST

Fast for one day this week. It can be just sunup to sundown, and you can even do the Daniel fast—fruit, vegetables, and water only. Let this be a physical and tangible reminder of what's real. It may make you feel weak or distracted or like you have less energy. Use these feelings as reminders to affix your attention on what is everlasting.

❧ NOTES

_____

_____

_____

_____

_____

_____

_____

_____

_____

_____

_____

_____

_____

_____

_____

_____

_____

_____

_____

7 | THE END

ᐁ INTRODUCTION

When we left Daniel, the kingdom of Babylon had fallen to the Medes and King Darius, but that wasn't the last word for the Israelites. They endure several more kings and their kingdoms before being allowed to return to Jerusalem from their exile. But even then, their story is far from over. They will face more confusion, more rescuing, more conquering, and more freedom before they reach the end. They will see Jesus, the Son of God, in the flesh. They will encounter changes to their religious rituals. They will be ruled by the government of Rome.

And, in fact, Rome is still in charge when we finally catch up with John in the book of Revelation. But nobody has forgotten Babylon, and John capitalizes on the long memory of the Israelites to impart the wisdom of Revelation. He uses Babylon as a metaphor for Rome because the alluring spirit of Babylon is alive and well in Rome. But, before the story ends, John has something to tell us about the future of Babylon, of Rome, and of our world today.

{ **Revelation 18**
Revelation 21

What do you learn about the character of God?

What do you learn about what God is up to in the world—both in the world of Scripture and in our world today?

How can we join God's work in the world?

∽ BREATHE IN THE WORD

Revelation 18:9, 11, 15, 19. Remember the exiles weeping by the river in Psalm 137 and consider whether you identify more with them or with the residents of Babylon weeping at the city's destruction. Where can you see God's presence in the experience of both kinds of people?

Revelation 21:24. What does it mean that "the kings of the earth will bring their glory into" the new city?

Revelation 18, 21. What parallels do you see between chapter 18 and chapter 21?

ꙩꙩ PRAYER

Redemptive God of grace, I claim your presence in my experiences—both as I weep by the river during exile and as I weep for the crumbling of my own kingdoms. You are with me always. I ask for your wisdom as I seek to bring your kingdom into the walls of Babylon. Show me the specific places where I can join your redemption in my areas of influence.

∾ MEDITATE

We live in the constant tension of being set apart from Babylon but called to give ourselves for her. Many theologians talk about this as the "already/not yet" tension. God is working in the world, and God is asking us to join this work. But the redeemed kingdom is not yet fully realized.

How have you seen God already taking the work of our hands, redeeming it, and bringing new life into the cracks of the crumbling kingdom? Take some time this week to tune into the redemption and renewal you see happening in the world—and ascribe these things to God, the Author of everything that is true, lovely, and beautiful.

∾ CHALLENGE: RENEW

What would it look like for you to bring renewal to your day-to-day routine? We must first recognize the new work God is doing in us before we begin to bring that work into the world. Where can you make space in your day to see God working in and around you?

Take time at the end of each day this week to think back and remember where you saw God that day. It can be something as simple as smelling flowers on the breeze, or pausing before responding in frustration to a coworker or loved one.

It might be difficult at first to recall moments in your day where you have noticed God working. But as you train yourself to tune in to God's presence throughout the day, you'll notice more and more moments where God is working in your life and in the world around you.

NOTES

~

_____

_____

_____

_____

_____

_____

_____

_____

_____

_____

_____

_____

_____

_____

_____

_____

_____

_____

Video sessions are available for individual purchase and download at www.BreatheSeries.com.

NOTES